101 Things To Do With Grits

101 Things To Do With Grits

BY HARRISS COTTINGHAM

Wyrick & Company

CHARLESTON

First Edition
10 09 08 07 06   20 19 18 17 16 15 14 13 12 11 10 9 8 7 6 5 4 3 2 1

Published by
Wyrick & Company
an imprint of Gibbs Smith, Publisher
P.O. Box 667
Layton, Utah 84041

Orders: 1.800.748.5439
www.gibbs-smith.com

Designed by Kurt Wahlner
Printed and bound in Korea

Library of Congress Cataloging-in-Publication Data

Cottingham, Harriss.
101 things to do with grits / Harriss Cottingham.—1st ed.
p. cm.
ISBN 0-941711-89-7 (alk. paper)
1. Cookery (Corn) 2. Grits. I. Title. II. Title: One hundred one
things to do with grits.

TX809.M2C68 2006
641.6'567—dc22

2006007925

This book is dedicated to my grandfather, Arthur Cottingham, with whom I began my apprenticeship in the kitchen at age five. He schooled me in the art of home cooking at our Sunday meal.

I also owe a tremendous debt of gratitude to my wife, Mary, for all her help and support in the process of writing this book. A special thanks to Rion Smith for being there on those late evenings and pushing me through on the keyboard. And last, but certainly not least, cheers to all my friends and family who love spending time in my kitchen.

CONTENTS

Ground Grits with Southern Caviar 62 • Shrimp & Scallop Scampi 63 • Farm-Raised Quail with Mushroom Gravy 64 • Grilled Tuna Steaks 65 • Thai Red Curry 66 • Black and Blue Grits 67 • Crab & Grits Cake Burger 68 • Hickory Smoked Chicken 69 • Baked Maple Grits with Country Ham 70 • Short Ribs with Cheddar Cheese Grits 71 • Apple Blossom Grits and Roasted Pork Loin 72 • Chicken Burrito with Chipotle Grits 73 • Barbecued Shrimp and Grits Souffle 74 • Grits and Crawfish 75 • Veggie Grits Chili 76 • Gouda Shrimp and Grits 77

Side Dishes
Roasted Corn and Sun-Dried Tomatoes 80 • Jalapeno and Bacon Grits 81 • Bacon and Jalapeno Fried Grits Squares 82 • Parmesan-Encrusted Grits Croutons 83 • Roasted Jalapeno-and-Cherry Stuffing 84 • Green Onion Cheesy Biscuits 85 • Ma Ethel's Mixed Bread 86 • Cheese Bread 87 • Stuffed Bell Peppers 88 • Grits & Black Beans 89• Big R's Barbecue Grits 90 • Vidalia Onion Casserole 91 • Very Garlicky Grits Casserole 92 • Panhandle Grits 93 • Extra Cheese Grits Souffle 94 • Baked Gruyere Grits Casserole 95

Desserts
Caramel Grits 98 • Southern Chocolate Grits Truffles 99 • Vanilla Bean Brûlée 100 • White Chocolate Brûlée 101 • Espresso Grits Brûlée 102 • Chocolate Grits and Sweet Waffles 103 • Buttermilk Waffles 104 • Orange and Maple Cream Pudding 105 • Fried Chocolate Grits 106 • Seasonal Berry Crepe 107 • Grits Neapolitan 108 • Hazelnut Trifle 109 • Key Lime Trifle 110 • Hazelnut Grits Napoleon 111 • Rum Raisin and Banana Porridge 112 • Tiramisu 113 • Strawberry Shortcakes 114 • Chocolate Cream Cheese Cake 115 • Grits with Tart Granny Smith Apples 116 • Strawberry Grits with Balsamic Reduction 117

Hominy Grits
Boiled Hominy 120 • Fried Hominy 121 • Hominy Casserole 122 • Southwest Baked Hominy 123

HELPFUL HINTS

I. Any flavored grits can be prepared ahead of time and stored for up to 5 days, as long as they are to be used in a cold recipe. Reheating could result in separation because of the heavy cream and butter used in most recipes.

2. It is best not to reheat grits, as you are trying to maintain a smooth, creamy consistency. Once you practice the basic recipes they shouldn't take long.

3. Instant grits can be substituted in any recipe to shorten preparation time. Follow the package directions.

4. When preparing grits from scratch, liberal use of cream and butter, although not standard in a low-fat recipe, always makes the dish smoother.

5. Always use a nonstick pot in preparation of grits recipes. My favorite brand is available at www.berndes.com.

6. Always use wooden utensils in the preparation of grits recipes and in any nonstick cookware to preserve the nonstick coating.

7. Always put grits pots in warm soapy water immediately after use for ease in cleanup. Do not put nonstick pots in the dishwasher.

8. Fresh herbs that are not used immediately after picking or purchase can be stored for up to a week in a damp paper towel in the refrigerator.

9. Fresh milk, cream, and butter should always be added toward the end of cooking time to prevent curdling.

10.To avoid burning grits on the bottom of pot, maintain medium-low heat once all liquids have been reduced.

11. Anson Mills organic stone-ground grits have the best flavor and consistency. I use them in any recipe that calls for stone-ground grits. Order them at www.ansonmills.com.

12. Adding grits to boiling water causes them to clump. To avoid this problem, add grits to cold water and bring them to a boil. (This hint is courtesy of my mother, Patty Honey).

13. Clarify butter in the microwave: Place I stick butter at a time in a microwave-safe dish. Cover with wax paper and microwave at 100 percent power for $1^{1}/_{4}$ to $1^{1}/_{2}$ minutes until melted. Let stand, uncovered, for 2–3 minutes until the solids settle, then gently pour off the clarified liquid. Repeat to get the amount of clarified butter needed.

14. To toast nuts, place shelled nuts in a single layer in a frying pan over medium-high heat. Stir or shake nuts continually until they start to turn golden, about 5–7 minutes.

BASIC GRITS

WHITE STONE-GROUND GRITS

2 cups **chicken broth***
I cup **white stone-ground grits**
4 tablespoons **butter**
1 1/2 cups **heavy cream**
salt and pepper

In a nonstick pot, combine chicken broth and grits. Bring to a boil and cook for 3 minutes, stirring constantly. Turn to medium-low heat, stir in butter and reduce liquid by half. As liquid reduces, add heavy cream in three to four additions, stirring occasionally. Entire process should take 45–60 minutes. When liquid is reduced, season with salt and pepper to taste. Makes 4 servings.

*This will provide the richest flavor, but water or organic vegetable broth can be used in its place.

YELLOW STONE-GROUND GRITS

2 cups **chicken broth***
1 cup **yellow stone-ground grits**
4 tablespoons **butter**
1$^1/_2$ cups **heavy cream**
salt and pepper

In a nonstick pot, combine chicken broth and grits. Bring to a boil and cook for 3 minutes, stirring constantly. Turn to medium-low heat, stir in butter and reduce liquid by half. As liquid reduces, add heavy cream in three to four additions, stirring occasionally. Entire process should take 45–60 minutes. When liquid is reduced, season with salt and pepper to taste. Makes 4 servings.

*This will provide the richest flavor, but water or organic vegetable broth can be used in its place.

INSTANT GRITS DONE RIGHT

1 cup **uncooked instant grits**
2 cups **chicken** or **vegetable broth**
1 stick **butter**
2 teaspoons **kosher salt**
2 teaspoons **black pepper**
3 dashes **Tabasco sauce**

Place broth in a nonstick pot and add grits. Cook grits according to package directions. Add butter, salt, pepper, and Tabasco sauce. Mix and serve. Makes 4–6 servings.

FLAVORED GRITS

TRUFFLE-SCENTED GRITS

1 tablespoon **butter**
1 cup **finely chopped portobello**
   mushrooms
2 teaspoons **white truffle oil**
   White Stone-Ground Grits
   (see page 12)

In a frying pan, brown butter and saute mushrooms over high heat for 2–3 minutes or until soft. Stir together oil, sauted mushrooms, and grits. Makes 4 servings.

SAVORY GRITS

$^1/_4$ cup **packed fresh, aromatic thyme leaves**
(no stems)
White Stone-Ground Grits
(see page 12)

Wash, stem, and scrape the thyme leaves with a sharp knife to bruise them (this releases their oils). Add to cooked grits to enhance the flavor and complement a wide variety of dishes. Makes 4 servings.

VARIATION: Substitute thyme with rosemary, parsley, oregano, or a mixture of these herbs but never more than $^1/_4$ cup to one 4-serving basic recipe.

PESTO-FLAVORED GRITS

4 cups	**tightly packed basil leaves,** washed and stemmed
	juice of 1 lemon
1 1/2 cups	**olive oil,** divided
5 cloves	**garlic,** finely chopped
1 cup	**toasted pine nuts**
2	**anchovy fillets**
1 cup	**grated Parmesan Reggiano**
	kosher salt and pepper
	White Stone-Ground Grits (see page 12)

In a blender or food processor, blend together basil, lemon juice, and
1/2 cup olive oil. While blending, add garlic, pine nuts, anchovies, and
cheese. Slowly add remaining olive oil to emulsify, and then salt and
pepper to taste.

Stir 1/2 cup of the pesto mixture at a time into warm grits, depending on
personal taste and desired strength. Makes 4 servings.

ROASTED GARLIC-INFUSED GRITS

$^1/_2$ cup **whole garlic cloves**
I cup **olive oil**
White Stone-Ground Grits
(see page 12)

Preheat oven to 400 degrees.

Place garlic and oil in small oven-safe ramekin and cover with foil. Bake for 45 minutes or until cloves are golden brown and softened. Strain and reserve oil.

With a fork, mash cloves into warm cooked grits. Stir in $^1/_4$ cup (or to taste) of reserved garlic-infused oil. Makes 4 servings.

WHITE CHEDDAR CHEESE GRITS

White Stone-Ground Grits
(see page 12)
I cup **finely grated Vermont white cheddar cheese** (sharp, if you like)
I tablespoon **Tabasco sauce**
pinch white pepper

When grits are nearly ready, stir in cheese, Tabasco sauce, and pepper. Makes 4 servings.

STILTON BLUE CHEESE GRITS

White Stone-Ground Grits
(see page 12)
¹/₂ cup **crumbled Stilton blue cheese**
1 tablespoon **Worcestershire sauce**
pinch black pepper

When grits are nearly ready, stir in cheese, Worcestershire sauce, and pepper. Serve with a rare New York strip steak. Makes 4 servings.

CHIPOTLE GRITS

I can (7.5 ounces) **chipotle peppers**
I can (4.5 ounces) **chopped green chiles**
I tablespoon **apple cider vinegar**
I tablespoon **cocoa powder**
pinch kosher salt
Yellow Stone-Ground Grits
(see page 13)

In a blender or food processor, blend all ingredients except grits until smooth. While grits are hot, stir in chipotle mixture. Makes 4 servings.

RED CURRY GRITS

2 tablespoons	**red curry paste**
1 can (12 ounces)	**coconut milk**
6	**basil leaves,** finely chopped
	juice of 1 lime
2	**stalks lemongrass**
	White Stone-Ground Grits
	(see page 12)

In a bowl, combine curry paste and coconut milk with a whisk. Add basil leaves, lime juice, and lemongrass and heat over medium-high heat for 10 minutes.

Remove lemongrass and fold cooked grits into mixture. Reduce heat to medium-low and let coconut mixture absorb into grits. Makes 4 servings.

OLD BAY LEMON GRITS

White or **Yellow Stone-Ground Grits**
(see pages 12 and 13)
zest of 1 large lemon
juice of 1 lemon
2 tablespoons **Old Bay Seasoning**
2 tablespoons **Tabasco sauce**
kosher salt and pepper

After grits have cooked for just a few minutes and before adding the cream, add the lemon zest, lemon juice, and seasoning. Continue recipe as directed. When liquid has reduced, add Tabasco sauce and salt and pepper to taste. Makes 4 servings.

SWEET VANILLA GRITS

2 cups **sugar water** ($1\frac{1}{2}$ cups sugar to 2
cups water)
White Stone-Ground Grits
(see page 12)
2 cups **heavy cream**
1 **whole vanilla bean**
4 tablespoons **vanilla extract**
2 tablespoons **butter**

In a saucepan, combine sugar water and uncooked grits and bring to a
boil. Reduce heat to low and cook for 45–60 minutes.

In a separate saucepan, slowly simmer cream over medium heat. Slice
vanilla bean down center and scrape seeds from husk, adding them to
cream with vanilla bean stalk. Add vanilla extract and simmer for 30–45
minutes until cream becomes aromatic; reduce by one-fourth. Discard
the bean and then add mixture and butter to grits and stir. Makes 4
servings.

CHOCOLATE GRITS

2 cups **sugar water** (1 1/2 cups sugar to 2 cups water)
White Stone-Ground Grits*
(see page 12)
4 tablespoons **vanilla extract**
2 cups **heavy cream,** divided
1/2 cup **cocoa powder**
4 tablespoons **butter**
1/2 pound **Ghirardelli milk chocolate,** sliced into slivers

In a saucepan, combine sugar water, vanilla extract, and uncooked grits. Bing to boil and reduce heat to low. Add 1 cup cream and cocoa powder to grits. Add additional cocoa, if necessary, to achieve rich, dark color. Add remaining cream, butter, and chocolate. Stir and cook on medium low until liquid is absorbed. Makes 4 servings.

*For a smoother texture, use instant grits.

PISTACHIO GRITS

2 cups **sugar water** (1 1/2 cups sugar
to 2 cups water)
White Stone-Ground Grits
(see page 12)
4 tablespoons **vanilla extract**
1/2 cup **shelled toasted pistachio nuts,**
ground fine in a food processor
4 tablespoons **butter**
4 tablespoons **pistachio syrup** or **extract**
2 cups **heavy cream**

In a saucepan, bring sugar water and uncooked grits to boil. Reduce
heat to low. Add vanilla, nuts, butter, and flavoring. As grits absorb liquid, add cream in two additions, stirring occasionally. Cook 45 minutes
on low or until liquid is absorbed. Makes 4 servings.

HAZELNUT GRITS

$^1/_2$ cup **shelled toasted hazelnuts,** ground fine
in a food processor
2 cups **sugar water** (1 $^1/_2$ cups sugar
to 2 cups water)
White Stone-Ground Grits
(see page 12)
4 tablespoons **vanilla extract**
4 tablespoons **butter**
4 tablespoons **hazelnut syrup** or **extract**
2 cups **heavy cream**

While hot, place toasted hazelnuts in a kitchen dishtowel and roll
together to remove bitter outer skin. Grind in a food processor and set
aside.

In a saucepan, combine sugar water and uncooked grits. Bring to a boil
and reduce heat to low. Add vanilla, nuts, butter, and flavoring. As
grits absorb liquid, add cream in two additions, stirring occasionally
until liquid is absorbed. Makes 4 servings.

STRAWBERRY GRITS

I cup **instant grits**
I teaspoon **strawberry extract**
2 tablespoons **unsalted butter**
I cup **chopped fresh strawberries**
$^1/_2$ cup **granulated sugar**

Prepare grits according to package directions and add extract.

In a frying pan, heat butter over medium-high heat, and once foam dissipates, add strawberries and sugar. Cook for 4–6 minutes, or until sugar has melted into a nice amount of strawberry syrup. Set aside to cool. Once grits have cooled, puree strawberries and syrup in a blender and fold into grits. Makes 4–6 servings.

KEY LIME GRITS

I cup	**water**
I cup	**key lime juice**
I cup	**instant grits**
4 tablespoons	**vanilla extract**
2 cups	**heavy cream**
I whole	**vanilla bean**
2 tablespoons	**butter**

In a pot, combine water, lime juice and grits. Bring to a boil and reduce heat to low. Cook for 15 minutes or until liquid is absorbed.

In a separate pot, add vanilla extract and cream. Bring to a slow simmer over medium heat. Slice vanilla bean down center and scrape seeds from husk into cream, adding vanilla bean stalk. Simmer for 30–45 minutes until cream becomes aromatic; reduce by one-fourth. Discard vanilla bean. Add mixture to grits and stir in butter. Makes 4–6 servings.

ESPRESSO GRITS

White Stone-Ground Grits
(see page 12) or **instant grits**
$^1/_2$ cup **cold espresso** or **very strong coffee**
$^1/_3$ cup **dark rum**

Prepare grits and then add espresso and rum. Let grits absorb liquid.
Makes 4–6 servings.

GOUDA GRITS

White Stone Ground-Grits
(see page 12)
1 cup **grated Gouda cheese**
1 tablespoon **Tabasco sauce**
pinch white pepper

When grits are nearly ready, add cheese, Tabasco sauce, and pepper. Stir, serve and enjoy. Makes 4 servings.

VARIATION: Substitute smoked Gouda for the Gouda to get a little different flavor.

BREAKFAST

SHRIMP AND GRITS WITH BACON AND CHEDDAR

2 cups	**Yellow** or **White Stone-Ground Grits** (see pages 12 and 13)
1 pound	**Carolina Pride thick-cut bacon**
1	**large sweet onion,** diced
4	**cloves garlic,** diced
1 pound (26–30)	**shrimp,** peeled (local fresh shrimp, when in season)
$^{1}/_{3}$ cup	**Worcestershire sauce**
$^{1}/_{4}$ cup	**white wine**
	Tabasco sauce
2 cups	**grated extra-sharp cheddar cheese,**

Pour cooked grits into 9 x 13-inch pan. Preheat oven to 350 degrees.

Cook bacon until crisp in a nonstick frying pan. Turn out onto paper towels and drain, reserving bacon grease in pan. Preheat frying pan to medium high and add reserved bacon grease. Caramelize onion and garlic until brown. Add shrimp and cook 3–5 minutes. Combine Worcestershire and wine and deglaze pan with liquid, stirring frequently. Reduce liquid by half or until slightly thickened. Remove from heat. Pour shrimp and onion mixture over grits. Season to taste with Tabasco sauce. Top with cheese, and then bake 15–20 minutes. Makes 4 servings.

OLD-FASHIONED SALMON AND GRITS

1 1/2 cans (14.5 ounces each) **pink salmon,** liquid reserved
2 **eggs**
1 tablespoon **olive oil**
1/4 cup **chopped onion**
1/4 cup **chopped green onion**
1/4 cup **chopped green bell pepper**
1 cup **grated sharp cheddar cheese**
salt and pepper
White Stone-Ground Grits
(see page 12)

Preheat oven to 350 degrees.

Break up salmon and drain, reserving 1/2 cup of remaining liquid. Combine eggs and salmon liquid and set aside. Preheat medium frying pan over medium-high heat. Add the olive oil, onions, and bell pepper, sauteing until onions and peppers are brown. Add salt and pepper to taste. Pour half the cooked grits into the bottom of a 13 x 9-inch greased pan. Then layer half the salmon, onion mixture, and cheese. Add remaining grits, then remaining salmon mixture, adding the remaining cheese and onion mixture last. Pour the egg mixture over top and bake 25–30 minutes. Makes 6–8 servings.

EGGS BENEDICT

Hollandaise sauce:

1 pound	**clarified unsalted butter**
6	**egg yolks**
$1/4$ cup	**white wine**
2 tablespoons	**white vinegar**
2 dashes	**Tabasco sauce**
	juice of 1 lemon
	white pepper and kosher salt
1 cup	**water**
	poaching liquid (3 quarts water, $1/2$ cup white vinegar, 1 tablespoon kosher salt)
$1/2$ pound	**Canadian bacon,** sliced
1 package	**English muffins**
1 dozen	**eggs**
	White or **Yellow Stone-Ground Grits** (see pages 12 and 13)

Preheat oven to 400 degrees. In a saucepan melt butter and then keep it warm. Whisk yolks in a stainless steel bowl. Add wine, vinegar, Tabasco, lemon juice, pepper and salt. Mix to incorporate all ingredients.

In a 2-quart saucepan or double boiler, bring 1 cup water to a soft boil. Place bowl with egg mixture on top. Whisk yolk mixture for 3–5 minutes. Do not stop. The yolks expand by whisking air into them. Avoid over-cooking yolks. Once mixture has a glossy look and is thick, remove from heat and slowly add melted butter in three additions, whisking constantly to incorporate. Keep sauce warm, but off direct heat.

Heat poaching liquid to 180 degrees or when small bubbles form on bottom of pan. Place Canadian bacon on a sheet pan and bake 15 minutes. Toast muffins and poach eggs. Place half a muffin on a plate. Top with grits, Canadian bacon, egg and Hollandaise sauce. Makes 12 servings.

SALMON AND GRITS TERRINE

1 pound **fresh salmon fillet**
3 sprigs **fresh dill**
3 stems **fresh tarragon**
3 stems **fresh thyme**
5 tablespoons **butter,** divided
2 bunches **scallions,** chopped
1 **loaf pan**
parchment paper
White Stone-Ground Grits
(see page 12)

Preheat oven to 400 degrees. Bake salmon about 12–16 minutes, or until fish flakes to the touch. Let salmon cool and then break into small pieces in a bowl. Chop all herbs finely, discarding any woody stems, and mix with salmon. Pour 4 tablespoons melted butter over salmon-and-herb mixture. Saute scallions in a tablespoon of butter until browned.

Line loaf pan with parchment paper, getting it as smooth as possible. Pour small amount of cooked grits into loaf pan, and then top with salmon mixture and scallions. Repeat layering until all ingredients have been used. Cover with parchment paper and refrigerate for 4 hours to set. Remove from refrigerator and un-mold. Cut into $^3/_4$-inch slices and serve. Makes 6–8 servings.

COUNTRY HAM
AND REDEYE GRAVY

$1/4$ cup **unsalted butter**
$1/2$ pound **country-style ham**
$1/2$ cup **coffee**
$1/4$ cup **boiling water**
2–3 dashes **Cholula hot sauce**
White Stone-Ground Grits
(see page 12)

Preheat a large cast-iron frying pan to medium-high heat. Melt butter and fry ham on each side for 2–3 minutes, turning ham only once, and then place on a serving platter. Deglaze frying pan with a mixture of coffee and boiling water, making sure to scrape the pan for all drippings. Cook for about 3–5 minutes to boiling, or when mixture reduces by one-fourth. Remove from heat and add hot sauce. Serve cooked grits with a small indentation in the top for Redeye Gravy accompanied by ham. Makes 6–8 servings.

BISCUITS WITH SAUSAGE AND GRITS GRAVY

I pound	**spicy sausage**
I bag	**frozen buttermilk biscuits**
2 packages	**sausage gravy mix**
2 tablespoons	**coarse ground black pepper**
	White Stone-Ground Grits (see page 12)
I pinch	**kosher salt**
4–6	**eggs**

In a frying pan, crumble sausage and cook until browned. Bake the biscuits according to package directions and set aside. Prepare gravy according to package directions and mix with sausage. Stir gravy into cooked grits until incorporated. Serve over biscuits with eggs cooked to order. Season with salt and pepper to taste. Makes 4–6 servings.

VEGGIE OMELETS

I dozen	**large eggs**
	kosher salt and pepper
2 dashes	**Tabasco sauce**
2 stems	**fresh rosemary,** chopped
3 stems	**fresh thyme,** chopped
³/₄ cup	**heavy cream**
I	**red onion,** diced
I bunch	**asparagus**
¹/₂ cup	**sliced fresh mushrooms**
I	**red pepper,** julienned
I	**green pepper,** julienned
¹/₄ cup	**butter,** cut into tablespoons
	White Cheddar Cheese Grits
	(see page 20)
I cup	**grated white cheddar cheese**

In a large bowl, mix eggs, salt, pepper, Tabasco sauce, rosemary, thyme, and heavy cream. Mix well, about 6 minutes. Preheat a frying pan to high heat, add a tablespoon of butter and saute onion until brown. Break asparagus in half. Add asparagus, mushrooms, and peppers to onion and cook until just tender. Divide veggies into 6–8 equal portions.

Heat a nonstick frying pan to medium high and place a tablespoon of butter in the pan. Ladle out about 4 ounces egg mixture into pan. Using a rubber spatula, scrape edges of pan, allowing eggs to cook. Once most of the eggs are cooked, add a layer of grits on half of the omelet, top with one portion veggies and fold over, browning each side of the omelet. Garnish with cheese. Makes 6–8 servings.

CORNED BEEF GRITS HASH

1	**Spanish onion,** diced
2	**garlic cloves,** minced
1/4 cup	**butter**
2 cups	**diced cooked corned beef**
2 tablespoons	**stone-ground mustard**
scant pinch	**ground nutmeg**
1 tablespoon	**dried Italian spices**
	White Stone-Ground Grits
	(see page 12)
8–12 eggs	**eggs**
4–6 pieces	**toast**

In a frying pan, cook onions and garlic in 2 tablespoons butter until browned. Add corned beef, mustard, and spices. Cook for about 2–3 minutes so ingredients incorporate well. In a bowl, mix together cooked grits and beef mixture. Refrigerate at least 3 hours.

Preheat a large cast-iron frying pan to medium-high heat, add half the remaining butter to coat, and press hash mixture into pan, molding mixture to form of pan. Shake pan to prevent sticking. Brown hash on each side. Remove from heat. Place a plate on top of pan and flip hash onto plate. Serve with eggs and toast. Makes 4–6 servings.

SWEET PORRIDGE
WITH FRESH FRUIT

fresh fruit (blackberries, raspberries,
  strawberries, or any fruit you like)
Sweet Vanilla Grits
  (see page 25)
$1/4$ cup **cold cream**
$1/2$ cup **packed brown sugar**

Wash and slice fruit, as needed. In a small bowl, add a portion of grits
and top with fruit, cream, and brown sugar. Makes 4–6 servings.

CHIPOTLE OMELETS

Chipotle Grits (see page 22)
1 dozen **eggs**
salt and pepper
3 dashes **Tabasco sauce**
chopped sage
³/₄ cup **heavy cream**
¹/₄ cup **butter,** cut into tablespoons
1 jar (12 ounces) **roasted red peppers,** sliced
1 can (7.5 ounces) **chipotle peppers,** sliced
1 cup **grated spicy jack cheese**

In a large bowl, mix eggs with salt, pepper, Tabasco sauce, sage, and cream. Mix well, about 6 minutes.

Heat a nonstick frying pan to medium-high heat and place 1 tablespoon butter in the pan. Ladle about 6 ounces of egg mixture. Using a rubber spatula, scrape edges of pan, allowing eggs to cook. Once most of the eggs are cooked, add a layer of grits on half the omelet. Place a portion of peppers and then cheese on top of grits, fold over and brown on both sides and serve with hash browns and fresh fruit. Makes 4–6 servings.

TOMATO BASIL QUICHE

	White Stone-Ground Grits (see page 12)
1 dozen	**eggs**
1 1/2 cups	**heavy cream**
	salt and pepper
2 ounces	**basil,** washed and cut fine
1 pint (8 ounces)	**cherry tomatoes,** halved
1/4 cup	**balsamic vinegar**
2	**deep-dish pie shells**
1 cup	**crumbled tomato basil feta cheese**

Preheat oven to 375 degrees.

In a bowl, mix eggs, cream, salt, and pepper. In a separate bowl, mix basil, tomatoes, and vinegar and toss with salt and pepper to taste. Divide vegetable mixture between two pie shells and then top with feta. Mix half the grits with eggs and pour mixture into pie shells, dividing between the two. Bake on middle rack for 30 minutes. Rotate quiche a full turn and bake another 15 minutes or until firm and browned on top. Makes 6 servings.

Appetizers

STUFFED MUSHROOMS

2 pounds **baby portobello mushrooms,** stemmed
Truffle-Scented Grits (see page 16)
I log **pepper-encrusted goat cheese,** crumbled

Preheat oven to 350 degrees.

Clean mushrooms with fine brush to remove dirt, or lightly wash without allowing them to absorb water. Fill each mushroom cap with a spoonful of grits and then top with goat cheese. Arrange each cap on baking sheet. Bake for 30–45 minutes, or until mushrooms are soft to touch. Makes 6–8 servings.

HOT CAJUN CRAB DIP

I can (8 ounces) **lump blue crabmeat**
I can (8 ounces) **crab claw meat**
Old Bay Lemon Grits (see page 24)
I cup **grated sharp cheddar cheese**
I tablespoon **Old Bay Seasoning**

Preheat oven to 350 degrees.

In a bowl, mix together crabmeat and crab claw meat. Fold into cooked grits. Place in an oven-safe baking dish and sprinkle with cheese. Bake for 45 minutes. Remove from oven and garnish with Old Bay Seasoning. Serve with your favorite crackers. Makes 4–6 servings.

ROASTED GARLIC
AND CHIVE TERRINE

1 bunch	**thin asparagus**
	Roasted Garlic–Infused Grits
	(see page 19)
2 bunches	**chives,** chopped
1 jar (12 ounces)	**roasted red peppers**

Trim and blanch asparagus. Layer grits, chives, asparagus, and red peppers in loaf pan lined with plastic wrap. Repeat until pan is full. Press ingredients into mold. Cover and chill for 4–6 hours. Remove from mold and cut into $1/4$-inch slices. Makes 6–8 servings.

SPINACH AND ARTICHOKE DIP

Roasted Garlic–Infused Grits
(see page 19)
juice of 1 lemon
$^1/_2$ cup **mayonnaise**
1 $^1/_2$ cups **Parmesan cheese**
$^1/_4$ cup **sour cream**
1 $^1/_2$ cans (14.5 ounces each) **artichokes,** drained and diced
1 package (8 ounces) **frozen spinach,** thawed and drained

Preheat oven 400 degrees.

In a bowl, add all ingredients to cooked grits and mix well. Place in oven-safe dish and bake for 45 minutes. Serve hot with pita chips. Makes 4–6 servings.

PESTO TOAST POINTS WITH BEEF TENDERLOIN

	juice of 2 lemons
2 tablespoons	**white vinegar**
¹/₂ cup	**olive oil,** divided
1 tablespoon	**Worcestershire sauce**
1 pound	**high-quality beef tenderloin,** center cut and trimmed
	fresh cracked coarse pepper
	kosher salt
1	**French baguette,** sliced ¹/₄-inch thick
3 tablespoons each	**chopped fresh thyme, parsley and rosemary**
	Pesto-Flavored Grits (see page 18)
¹/₄ cup	**grated Parmesan Reggiano**

Combine lemon juice, vinegar, ¹/₄ cup oil and Worcestershire sauce in a plastic zipper-lock bag with beef. Refrigerate for at least 2 hours. Remove beef from bag and generously coat with salt and pepper. Sear beef over high heat on all sides, about 1 minute per side or 3–5 minutes total. Place in freezer for 2 hours.

Preheat oven to 350 degrees. Place baguette slices in large mixing bowl and coat with remaining olive oil, herbs and a pinch of salt and pepper. Bake on baking sheet for 12–15 minutes, or until golden brown.

Remove beef from freezer and slice paper-thin. Place slices between two layers of plastic wrap. Pat lightly with a medium serving spoon until meat becomes very thin. Spoon pesto grits onto toast points. Top with beef and garnish with cheese.

SALMON AND GRITS CAKES

	Old Bay Lemon Grits (see page 24)
2 pounds	**smoked salmon**
1 1/2 cups	**House-Autry Seafood Breader**
2 tablespoons	**butter**
2 tablespoons	**vegetable oil**
I container (8 ounces)	**sour cream**
I large	**red onion,** diced fine
	chives, for garnish

Let grits cool to room temperature. Break up salmon and add to grits.
Pat grits mixture into small pancake-like patties. Coat patties with
seafood breader and pan saute in butter and oil until crisp and golden
brown. Serve with a dollop of sour cream, diced onion, and a few
chives. Makes 4–6 servings.

SOUTHWESTERN SEVEN-LAYER DIP

Chipotle Grits (see page 22)
2 cans (8 ounces each) **refried beans**
16 ounces **sour cream**
16 ounces **guacamole dip**
1 jar (8 ounces) **salsa**
1 cup **grated sharp cheddar cheese**
1 cup **grated pepper jack cheese**
1 jar (8 ounces) **pickled jalapenos**
1 small can (4.5 ounces) **black olives,** sliced
3 cans (4 ounces each) **diced green chiles**

Layer ingredients in order as listed above in a round platter and chill for
2 hours. Serve with chips, lime, and cold beer. Makes 8–10 servings.

FRIED SHRIMP AND GRITS BALLS

8 ounces **peeled tiger shrimp,** washed and chopped into small pieces

3 tablespoons **butter**

6 ounces **pickled jalapeno peppers**

White Stone-Ground Grits (see page 12)

5 cups **vegetable oil**

House-Autry Seafood Breader

kosher salt and pepper

Saute shrimp in a hot pan with butter and salt and pepper until firm. Stir shrimp and jalapenos into the cooked grits. Pour shrimp-and-grit mixture onto a sheet pan and let cool to room temperature; place in refrigerator for 4–6 hours.

Bring oil to 375 degrees in a frying pot or deep fryer. Make $1/2$-inch balls out of the cold grits, coat evenly with seafood breader, and fry 5 to 8 balls at a time, depending on how big the fryer is, until golden brown with a crispy outside.

Serve with cocktail sauce or use as a side item with an entree. They go great with low-country red rice and good southern coleslaw. Makes 4–6 servings.

GRITS MAKI

4 bunches	**collard greens**
2	**Granny Smith apples,** peeled and cut into small pieces
6 pack	**Heineken beer**
	kosher salt and pepper
12 ounces	**pickled ginger**
1 jar (2 ounces)	**wasabi powder**
1 pound	**boiled shrimp** (use an Old Bay Seasoning bag in your water)
	White Stone-Ground Grits (see page 12)
2	**cucumbers,** peeled, seeded and cut into long thin strips
4	**roma tomatoes,** seeded and julienned

Cut ribs out of collards. Discard ribs and mix greens with apples. Place mixture into a stockpot and add 5 beers (you can drink the remaining one!) with two pinches kosher salt, half the ginger, and all the ginger juice. Bring collards to a boil and boil for 5 minutes. Reduce heat to medium-low, cook for 1 hour, or until tender. Let cool.

Make wasabi paste by following directions on wasabi powder jar. Stir 1 1/2 tablespoons paste into cooked grits.

Peel shrimp; slice in half lengthwise. Place greens one piece at a time onto cutting board and overlap until there is a 2 x 6-inch sheet of greens. Place a layer of wasabi grits on collards and spread evenly. Place 4 strips of cucumbers, 6 strips of tomato, and 6 pieces of shrimp down middle of roll. Place small amount of mixed wasabi paste on the outside edge of the roll. Roll outside edge into middle and finish by rolling through; make sure to roll it tight. Chill roll for 1 hour, cut into 6–8 pieces. Serve with ginger, wasabi, and soy sauce. Makes 6–8 servings.

*Recipe courtesy of Executive Chef Craig Fincher.

SAUSAGE DIP

1 package (8 ounces) **cream cheese,** at room temperature
1 can (8 ounces) **Rotel tomatoes**
White Stone-Ground Grits (see page 12)
1 pound **spicy sausage**
2 tablespoons **butter**
1 teaspoon **ground thyme**
1 teaspoon **ground sage**

Add cream cheese and tomatoes to hot grits. Cook sausage in nonstick saute pan with butter; add thyme and sage. When cooked through, stir together with grits. Serve with choice of crackers, corn chips, or toast points. Makes 4–6 servings.

VELVEETA MEXICAN DIP

I pound	**Velveeta Mexican cheese**
I can (8 ounces)	**Rotel tomatoes**
I can (4.5 ounces)	**green chiles**
$^1/_4$ cup	**salsa**
	Yellow Stone-Ground Grits (see page 13)
I bag	**tortilla chips**

Melt cheese and mix well with tomatoes, chiles, and salsa. Add mixture to cooked grits in two additions, mixing well each time. Serve hot with tortilla chips. Makes 4–6 servings.

VARIATION: Add I jar (12 ounces) roasted red peppers, diced.

ENTREES

ROASTED PORK LOIN
WITH APPLE COMPOTE

2 tablespoons	**butter**
3	**large tart apples,** peeled and sliced into small pieces
1/4 cup	**brown sugar**
1	**small goat cheese log**
2 pounds	**pork tenderloin** or **pork roast** **kosher salt and pepper**
1 teaspoon	**garlic powder**
1 teaspoon	**cumin**
1 teaspoon	**onion powder**
	Chipotle Grits (see page 22)

Preheat oven to 400 degrees.

Heat a frying pan to high heat, add butter, let foam stop, and then add apples and brown sugar, cooking until apples are soft. Add goat cheese, reduce to medium heat, and mix until well incorporated. Set aside. Place pork on a safe surface and coat with dry ingredients. Braise all sides of pork in a hot pan to lock in flavor. Cook pork in oven until cooked through, or until it reaches an internal temperature of 160 degrees. Time will vary depending on the cut. Let pork rest for 10 minutes. Place grits in a serving dish and place sliced pork over the grits. Top with apple compote. Makes 4–6 servings.

PAN-FRIED LOBSTER TAILS

3 large **lobster tails**
1 cup **House-Autry Seafood Breader**
$^1/_4$ cup **butter**
Old Bay Lemon Grits (see page 24)
1 can (16 ounces) **lobster claw meat**
5 stems **fresh lemon thyme,** chopped

Remove lobster meat from shell and lightly bread with seafood breader.

In a frying pan, melt butter on high heat, add lobster tails and fry until golden brown. Serve over grits. Toss claw meat in drippings to warm. Spoon drippings and meat over lobster tails. Garnish with fresh thyme. Makes 4–6 servings.

SEAFOOD PAELLA

$1/2$ cup **heavy cream**
$1/2$ cup **white wine**
2 big pinches **saffron**
kosher salt and pepper
6 ounces **clams**
6 ounces **green lip mussels**
$1/2$ pound **shrimp,** peeled
6 ounces **medium scallops**
I large **onion,** diced
I pound **spicy link sausage**
White Stone-Ground Grits (see page 12)
hot sauce

In a pot, bring cream and wine to simmer; add saffron, salt, and pepper.
Place all seafood in cream mixture and cook until shrimp float.

In a frying pan, brown onion, add sausage and cook through. Add
seafood mixture to onions and reduce by half. Stir mixture into grits
and serve with hot sauce to taste. Makes 4–6 servings.

OLD-TIMEY WHITE GRITS WITH MEATBALLS

White Stone-Ground Grits (see page 12) **or instant grits**
2 pounds **ground beef**
kosher salt and pepper
1 teaspoon **garlic powder**
$^1/_2$ cup **Worcestershire sauce,** divided
2$^1/_2$ tablespoons **butter**
$^1/_4$ cup **coffee**

If using instant grits, follow package directions.

In a bowl, combine beef, all dry ingredients, and 2 tablespoons Worcestershire sauce. Make meatballs to desired size.

In a frying pan, heat butter over medium-high heat and cook meatballs. Large meatballs may require a few minutes in oven at 350 degrees to finish cooking through. Serve meatballs over cooked grits. Deglaze pan with remaining Worcestershire and coffee. Cook and scrape down sides, reduce by one-fourth and spoon over meatballs. Makes 4–6 servings.

YELLOW STONE-GROUND GRITS WITH SOUTHERN CAVIAR

I can (8 ounces)	**white corn**
I can (8 ounces)	**black-eyed peas**
I jar	**roasted red peppers**
2	**garlic cloves,** minced
$^1/_2$	**red onion,** diced fine
I tablespoon	**whole grain mustard**
2 tablespoons	**white vinegar**
6 ounces	**spicy relish**
	Yellow Stone-Ground Grits (see page 13)

Drain corn and black-eyed peas in a fine mesh strainer, wash, and set aside. Chop peppers into small pieces and place all ingredients except grits in a large bowl, mix well and chill for at least I hour. After the Southern Caviar has chilled, cook grits and serve the caviar over top hot grits. Makes 4–6 servings.

SHRIMP & SCALLOP SCAMPI

3 tablespoons	**unsalted butter**
2 tablespoons	**vegetable oil**
I pound	**medium shrimp,** peeled (fresh if in season)
¹/₂ pound	**medium scallops**
2 large	**shallots,** minced
2	**garlic gloves,** minced
2 tablespoons	**finely chopped parsley**
2 sprigs	**fresh thyme,** steamed and chopped
	juice of I lemon
¹/₃ cup	**Sauvignon Blanc**
	Savory Grits (see page 17)

Heat a large skillet to medium high and add butter and oil. Add shrimp
and scallops. When shrimp starts to turn pink and scallops have
browned, turn them and add shallots, garlic, herbs, and liquids. Saute
for about 3 minutes more, or until scallops are firm on the outside and
liquid has reduced and thickened. Serve over grits while hot. Makes 4–6
servings.

FARM-RAISED QUAIL
WITH MUSHROOM GRAVY

2 cups	**grits** (your choice)
	kosher salt and pepper
4 tablespoons	**Lawry's Poultry Seasoning**
6	**fresh quail,** washed and dried (or substitute Cornish game hens or chicken breasts)
6 small	**sprigs fresh rosemary**
I stick	**unsalted butter,** room temperature and cut into small pieces
12 ounces	**fresh mushrooms,** cleaned and quartered
I cup	**Marsala cooking wine**

Prepare grits according to directions. Preheat oven to 400 degrees.

In a small bowl, mix 4 pinches kosher salt and 4 pinches pepper with poultry seasoning. Coat the quail evenly with this mixture. Put the rosemary inside the cavity of the bird. Bake I hour, or until internal temperature reaches 175 degrees. Remove from oven and let rest 10 minutes. While oven cools, cover and then place quail back in warm oven.

Heat a large frying pan over medium-high heat and add 2 tablespoons butter, let foam dissipate, and add mushrooms, sauteing until aromatic and browned. Deglaze pan with wine and bring to a boil, reducing by one-fourth. Remove from heat and add remaining butter a few pieces at a time, letting most of it melt before adding more. Do not put pan back on heat after adding butter because the butter and wine will separate. Serve quail with grits topped with mushrooms and gravy. Makes 6 servings.

GRILLED TUNA STEAKS

I tablespoon	**sesame oil**
I tablespoon	**chili oil**
$1/3$ cup	**sake**
3	**scallions,** cleaned and chopped
4 (6–8 ounce)	**tuna steaks** (sashimi grade if available)
I jar (2 ounces)	**wasabi powder**
	White Stone-Ground Grits (see page 12)

In a bowl, mix together oils, sake, and scallions. Marinate tuna steaks in mixture at least 2 hours. Spray grill with nonstick spray and heat. Light some coals (about $1/4$ of the bag) and let burn until they are very gray. Spread them evenly, scrape the grill grate, and then spray with nonstick spray away from the heat (spray will flame). Place grate on grill and let it get hot. If using a gas grill, heat to medium-high. Lightly spray tuna steaks and grill for I–2 minutes, rotate a quarter turn and then cook another minute; flip and repeat. Tuna is best served medium-rare, so it should still have a warm, pink center. Cooking time will be brief if done over a hot grill.

Make wasabi paste by following directions on wasabi powder jar. Stir I $1/2$ tablespoons paste into cooked grits.

Serve fish with wasabi grits. Makes 4 servings.

THAI RED CURRY

4	**chicken breasts**
	kosher salt and pepper
2 tablespoons	**olive oil**
2 tablespoons	**butter**
2 tablespoons	**vegetable oil**
3/4 pound	**fresh French green beans**
I	**red bell pepper,** julienned
I	**yellow bell pepper,** julienned
1/2 head	**white cabbage,** shredded
1/2 cup	**fresh basil,** julienned
1/4 cup	**ponzu sauce** (in the Asian food aisle)
	juice of I lime
3 pinches	**fresh cilantro,** for garnish
	Red Curry Grits (see page 23)*

Preheat oven to broil.

Sprinkle chicken with salt and pepper to taste, and then drizzle with olive oil. Cook chicken for about 45 minutes, flipping it halfway through (broil settings vary so watch chicken, as it may be done before the 45 minutes).

Preheat a large frying pan to high. Add butter and vegetable oil, let foam and then add vegetables, basil, and a pinch of kosher salt. Mix together and let sit for about 2 minutes and then stir, letting sit again. Vegetables should caramelize and release their sugars. Once vegetables have browned, reduce heat to medium-high; add ponzu and lime juice, stirring frequently for 5 minutes. Slice chicken and serve over grits, topped with vegetable mixture. Garnish with cilantro. Makes 4 servings.

*Green curry may be substituted.

BLACK AND BLUE GRITS

$^1/_4$ cup **Worcestershire sauce**
juice of 1 lemon
kosher salt and pepper
2 pounds **beef tenderloin,** whole and trimmed
2 tablespoons **vegetable oil**
8 ounces **fresh mushrooms,** cleaned and sliced
1 package **phyllo sheets**
2 sticks **unsalted butter,** melted
Stilton Blue Cheese Grits (see page 21)

Preheat oven to 350 degrees.

Mix Worcestershire and lemon juice together. Salt and pepper beef, and then let marinate in liquid for 1 hour. Heat a frying pan with oil and sear beef on all sides; remove beef from pan and then add mushrooms, cooking until aromatic.

Place 1 sheet phyllo on a flat clean surface. Using a basting brush, brush whole phyllo sheet with butter. Place another phyllo sheet on top and repeat this process with 7 sheets phyllo. Place beef in the middle on top of layered phyllo and top with mushrooms. Fold dough around beef, trimming off excess. Bake in oven for about 45 minutes, or until the internal temperature reaches 120 degrees (medium-rare). Remove from oven and let rest for 10 minutes. Serve with grits and a vegetable of your choice. Makes 4 servings.

CRAB & GRITS CAKE BURGER

	White Stone-Ground Grits (see page 12)
1 cup	**mayonnaise**
	juice of 1 lemon
1 tablespoon	**Old Bay Seasoning**
1 dash	**Worcestershire sauce**
1 tablespoon	**Tabasco sauce**
1/3 cup	**sour cream**
1 pound	**lump blue crabmeat**
1/3 cup	**Nabisco cracker meal**
2	**lemons,** zested
	juice of 2 lemons
1/3 cup	**chopped jalapenos**
1 cup	**House-Autry Seafood Breader**
1/4 cup	**vegetable oil**

Prepare grits according to recipe and then chill. Add first twelve ingredients, being careful not to break up crab. Form into 6 patties and bread with seafood breader. Pan fry over medium-high heat with oil until crisp and golden brown on both sides, about 2–3 minutes. Serve on a hamburger bun with toppings of your choice. Makes 6 servings.

HICKORY SMOKED CHICKEN

1 bag **hickory/mesquite wood chips** (at the grocery store on the charcoal aisle)
1 **chicken,** cut into legs, thighs, breasts, and wings
1 container **Montreal Chicken Seasoning**
1 pinch **kosher salt**
1 pinch **pepper**
Pesto-Flavored Grits (see page 18)

Soak 4 cups wood chips in water for at least 1 hour. Season chicken generously with seasoning, salt, and pepper. Light some charcoal for the grill. Once charcoal is ready, keep coals to one side. Place 2 cups drained wood chips on the coals and then cook chicken indirectly by placing on grill on the opposite side from the coals. Cover and let smoke for 30 minutes, then remove lid and rotate chicken. Add 1 more cup wood chips, cover, and then let smoke for 45 minutes, or until internal temperature reaches 175 degrees. Serve with grits. Makes 6 servings.

VARIATION: Although designed for a charcoal grill, this recipe can be prepared on a gas grill. Heat one side of the grill to medium-high and place wood chips on hot side. Then follow the directions above.

BAKED MAPLE GRITS WITH COUNTRY HAM

White Stone-Ground Grits (see page 12)
$^1/_2$ cup **Vermont maple syrup**
$^1/_3$ cup **tightly packed brown sugar**
I pound **high-quality country ham**

Prepare grits according to recipe and then add syrup. Preheat oven to 375 degrees.

Place grits in a casserole dish and sprinkle with brown sugar. Bake 15–20 minutes. or until brown sugar has melted. Heat a frying pan to medium-high heat. Fry ham until brown and crispy. Serve grits with ham. Makes 6 servings.

SHORT RIBS WITH CHEDDAR CHEESE GRITS

	White Cheddar Cheese Grits (see page 20)
5 pounds	**bone-in short ribs**
2 pinches	**kosher salt**
2 pinches	**pepper**
$^1/_2$ cup	**flour**
$^1/_2$ cup	**olive oil**
2	**yellow onions**
1 bag (12 ounces)	**baby carrots**
1 bag (8 ounces)	**petite green beans**
$^1/_2$ head	**white cabbage**
8$^1/_2$ cups	**red wine**
3 cups	**beef stock**
10 cloves	**garlic,** whole
5	**bay leaves**
4 sprigs	**thyme**
2 stems	**rosemary,** leafed and finely chopped

In a bowl, season ribs with salt and pepper and then toss with flour, mixing well. Add oil to large Dutch oven on medium-high heat. Brown ribs evenly, about 4–6 minutes. Remove ribs and cook vegetables in pan drippings for 4 minutes. Deglaze pan with half the wine, scraping down all sides and edges. Add beef stock and rest of wine. Add garlic cloves, bay leaves, thyme, and rosemary. Reduce wine and stock by one-third; add ribs back to mix and reduce heat to medium. Simmer for 1 hour, or until half the liquid has reduced. Serve grits in a bowl, topped with ribs and vegetables. Makes 6 servings.

APPLE BLOSSOM GRITS AND ROASTED PORK LOIN

Dry Rub for Pork:

2 tablespoons	**garlic powder**
I tablespoon	**pepper**
I tablespoon	**dried thyme**
¹/₂ tablespoon	**cayenne pepper**

	Yellow Stone-Ground Grits (see page 13)
I ¹/₂ cups	**organic apple juice**
2	**pork tenderloins**
3 tablespoons	**vegetable oil**
2	**Granny Smith apples,** peeled and sliced
I large	**red onion,** julienned
3 tablespoons	**olive oil**
	kosher salt and pepper

Prepare grits according to recipe but substitute organic apple juice in place of I ¹/₂ cups water. Preheat oven to 350 degrees.

In a bowl, mix all dry ingredients for the dry rub. Wash pork in cold water and pat dry with a paper towel. Place pork onto a platter and apply dry rub.

In a frying pan, heat vegetable oil to medium-high heat and sear pork on all sides. Toss apples and onion in a bowl with olive oil and salt and pepper to taste. Turn apple mixture out onto a roasting pan and place seared pork on top. Bake for 35–40 minutes, or until internal temperature reaches 160 degrees. Serve with grits and your favorite vegetable. Makes 6 servings.

CHICKEN BURRITO WITH CHIPOTLE GRITS

I batch	**Hickory Smoked Chicken** (see page 69)
	Chipotle Grits (see page 22)
I package	**10-inch tortillas**
4	**roma tomatoes,** chopped
I large	**onion,** chopped
I jar (12–16 ounces)	**salsa**
I can (4.5 ounces)	**chopped green chiles**
I head	**green-leaf lettuce,** cleaned and sliced into fine ribbons
2 cups	**grated cheese**
2 cups	**guacamole**

Prepare chicken according to recipe. Once it has cooled, pick chicken apart. Build burritos in tortillas using the cooked grits and the toppings of your choice. Heat the finished burrito in the microwave for about 30–45 seconds. Makes 8 servings.

BARBECUED SHRIMP AND GRITS SOUFFLE

Big R's Barbecue Grits (see page 90)
8 cups **water**
2 tablespoons **kosher salt**
1 **onion,** roughly chopped
juice of 1 lemon
1 pound **shrimp,** peeled and deveined
1 cup **heavy cream**
1 **egg**

Preheat oven to 375 degrees.

In a pot, bring water, salt, onion, and lemon to a boil. Add shrimp and cook until just pink, about 1 minute. Remove and cool in an ice bath. Strain, roughly chop and reserve.

In a bowl, combine cream and egg with a whisk. In a separate bowl, combine grits, cream mixture, and chopped shrimp. Transfer to a round casserole dish, filling about three-quarters to the top. Bake 30 minutes. Serve immediately. Makes 4–6 servings.

GRITS AND CRAWFISH

                    I large **onion,** diced
                         2   **shallots,** finely chopped
                         2   **garlic cloves,** diced
                 $^1/_2$ pound **ground spicy sausage**
                 $^1/_2$ cup   **cooking Marsala**
          1 $^1/_2$ pounds **crawfish tails**
                             Old Bay Lemon Grits (see page 24)

Preheat oven to 325 degrees.

Heat a frying pan to medium-high heat and then add onion, shallots, and garlic and saute until golden brown. Add sausage and cook for 7 minutes, or until cooked through. Deglaze pan with Marsala, and then add crawfish. Pour grits into a baking dish and top with crawfish mixture. Bake for 25 minutes. Makes 6 servings.

VEGGIE GRITS CHILI

I can (8 ounces)	**Rotel tomatoes**
2 cans (4.5 ounces each)	**chopped green chiles**
I box	**vegetarian chili mix**
10	**garlic cloves**
	White or **Yellow Stone-Ground Grits** (see pages 12 and 13)
$^1/_2$ cup	**sour cream**
I cup	**grated cheddar cheese**

Fold tomatoes and green chiles into cooked grits and cook over low heat until liquid has been absorbed. Cook veggie chili according to package directions, adding the garlic. When done, fold in grits. Serve with sour cream and top with cheese. Makes 8–10 servings.

76

GOUDA SHRIMP AND GRITS

$^1/_2$ pound	**bacon,** cooked and chopped into small pieces
I bunch	**green onions,** chopped in very small rounds
I large	**sweet onion,** diced
4	**cloves garlic,** diced
I pound (26–30)	**shrimp,** peeled (local fresh shrimp when in season)
$^1/_3$ cup	**Worcestershire sauce**
$^1/_4$ cup	**white wine**
	Gouda Grits (see page 32)
	Tabasco sauce
2 cups	**grated Gouda cheese**

Preheat oven to 350 degrees.

Cook bacon until crisp in a nonstick frying pan. Drain bacon on paper towels, reserving bacon grease in pan. Preheat frying pan to medium-high heat and add bacon grease. Add onions and garlic and caramelize until brown. Add shrimp and cook for 3–5 minutes. Combine Worcestershire and wine and then deglaze pan with liquid, stirring frequently. Reduce liquid by half, or until slightly thickened; remove from heat. Pour grits into a 9 x 13-inch baking dish. Pour shrimp and onion mixture over grits and add crumbled bacon. Use a dash of Tabasco to taste, top with cheese, and bake 15–20 minutes. Makes 6 servings.

SIDE DISHES

ROASTED CORN AND SUN-DRIED TOMATOES

I cup **sun-dried tomatoes,** julienned
2 cups **salt brine** (2 cups water mixed with 2 tablespoons kosher salt)
2 cups **yellow sweet corn**
1/4 cup **olive oil**
salt and pepper
I package (6 ounces) **fresh chevre cheese**
White Stone-Ground Grits (see page 12)

Preheat oven to 375 degrees.

Hydrate tomatoes in the salt brine for 30 minutes. While tomatoes are hydrating, toss corn with oil and salt and pepper to taste. Drain the tomatoes and add to corn mixture. Roast mixture in oven for 45 minutes or until brown. Remove from oven and stir into cooked grits. Add half of the crumbled cheese to grits. Use remaining cheese for garnish once grits are plated. Makes 4–6 servings.

JALAPENO AND BACON GRITS

White or **Yellow Stone-Ground Grits**
(see pages 12 and 13)
8 slices **thick-sliced bacon**
¹/₄ cup **pickled jalapeno slices**
salt and pepper
green Tabasco sauce

Slice bacon into thin strips and fry until crispy. Drain excess bacon grease and stir fried bacon into grits. Dice jalapeno slices and add to grit mixture. Stir thoroughly and add salt and pepper to taste. Garnish with a splash of green Tabasco. Makes 4–6 servings.

VARIATION: For a more spicy version, add more jalapenos. For less spicy, add fewer.

BACON AND JALAPENO FRIED GRITS SQUARES

Instant Grits Done Right (see page 14)
8 slices **thick-sliced bacon**
1/4 cup **pickled jalapeno slices**
salt and pepper
1 1/2 cups **House-Autry Seafood Breader**
8 cups **peanut oil**

Cook grits according to recipe. Slice bacon into thin strips and fry until crispy. Drain excess bacon grease and add fried bacon to grits. Dice jalapeno slices and stir into grits. Pour grit mixture into a 9 x 13-inch baking dish and spread evenly. Cover tightly and refrigerate for 3–6 hours until firm. Remove from refrigerator and cut grits into half-inch squares, making about 40–45 squares. Place seafood breader in a deep bowl. Carefully bread 5–6 squares at a time.

Preheat oil to 375 degrees in a deep fryer or on the stovetop in a fry-safe pot. Add 10–12 breaded grit squares to preheated oil. Fry until golden brown, about 4–6 minutes. Serve as an accompaniment to any low-country dish. Makes 6–8 servings.

PARMESAN-ENCRUSTED GRITS CROUTONS

Roasted Garlic–Infused Grits (see page 19)
1 cup **grated Parmesan cheese,** divided
1 tablespoon **Italian seasoning**
1 cup **House-Autry Seafood Breader**
8 cups **peanut oil**

Prepare grits according to recipe. Stir $^1/_2$ cup Parmesan into grits. Spread grit mixture evenly onto a half-size sheet pan. Cover and refrigerate for 3–6 hours until firm. Toss the remaining cheese and dry ingredients together in a bowl. Once grits are firm, cut into small crouton-size pieces and carefully coat with dry ingredient mixture.

Preheat oil to 375 degrees in a deep fryer or on stovetop in a fry-safe pot. Add 10–12 croutons to preheated oil. Fry until golden brown and crispy. Great with Caesar salads. Makes 6–8 servings.

ROASTED JALAPENO-
AND-CHERRY STUFFING

Yellow Stone-Ground Grits
(see page 13)
5 **fresh whole jalapenos**
1 cup **dried cherries**
$^1/_4$ cup **olive oil**
  salt and pepper
1 cup **uncooked stovetop stuffing**
4 sprigs **fresh rosemary,** chopped
$^1/_2$ stick **lightly salted butter**
1 **egg**
$^1/_2$ cup **milk**

Prepare grits according to recipe. Preheat oven to 350 degrees.

Cut off tops of jalapenos. Slice in half, core and de-seed. Toss jalapenos
and cherries in olive oil with a scant pinch of salt and pepper. In a
roasting pan, roast mixture in oven for 30–45 minutes. Remove from
oven and place on cutting board, coarse chop cherries and peppers and
set aside.

Place stuffing in a mixing bowl with rosemary, melted butter, egg, and
milk. Add jalapenos and cherries. Beat with fork. Fold in the stuffing,
then add grits in 4 additions, mixing thoroughly each time. Place in a
greased casserole dish, and bake for 45–50 minutes, or until golden
brown on top. Stuffing is especially good with pork tenderloin and col-
lard greens. Makes 6–8 servings.

GREEN ONION CHEESY BISCUITS

$3/4$ cup **dry instant grits**
I bunch **green onions,** finely chopped
2 tablespoons **brown sugar**
4 tablespoons **baking powder**
I $1/4$ cups **flour**
5 tablespoons **butter,** at room temperature
I cup **grated sharp Vermont white
cheddar cheese**
$1/2$ cup **milk**

Preheat oven to 425 degrees.

Brown onions in a frying pan with a tablespoon of butter for 7 minutes over medium-high heat, stirring frequently. Combine dry ingredients. Cut in remaining butter with a fork until mixture resembles coarse crumbs. Add cheese, onions, and milk. Mix until dry ingredients are moist and then knead 4–5 times on a floured surface. Roll out into 9-inch circles and then cut with a medium biscuit cutter or rim of a drinking glass. Place on a parchment-lined baking sheet, and cook 20–25 minutes, or until golden brown. Makes 6–8 servings.

MA ETHEL'S MIXED BREAD

I envelope	**yeast**
2 cups	**warm water**
2 tablespoons	**vegetable shortening**
2 tablespoons	**sugar**
2 teaspoons	**salt**
2 cups	**White or Yellow Stone-Ground Grits**
	(see pages 12 and 13)
4 cups	**flour**

In a bowl, dissolve yeast in warm water. Add shortening, sugar, salt, and cooked grits. Stir in enough flour to make a stiff batter. Cover and let rise until doubled in size. Knead with hands and divide into 2 well-greased loaf pans. Let rise until doubled in size. When ready to bake, preheat oven to 400 degrees and bake about 50 minutes. Makes 6–8 servings.

CHEESE BREAD

3 cups **bread flour,** divided
1 cup **uncooked instant grits**
1/4 cup **powdered milk**
1 tablespoon **yeast**
1 teaspoon **kosher salt**
1 **egg**
1/2 cup **vegetable oil**
2 cups **warm water**
1 cup **grated pepper jack cheese**
2 tablespoons **butter,** melted

Preheat oven to 350 degrees.

In a bowl, mix 2 cups of flour with grits, milk, yeast, and salt. In a separate bowl, combine egg, oil, and water. Stir into flour mixture until well blended. Add cheese and remaining flour as needed until dough comes together. Knead about 2–4 times on a floured surface. Place dough in a bowl, cover and let rise about 30 minutes. Punch down dough and place into a loaf pan; let rise again until double in size. Lightly brush top with melted butter and bake 30–45 minutes. Makes 6–8 servings.

STUFFED BELL PEPPERS

I small	**sweet onion,** diced
2 tablespoons	**vegetable oil**
$^1/_2$ pound	**ground sirloin**
I teaspoon	**garlic powder**
I teaspoon	**onion powder**
	salt and pepper to taste
I can (8 ounces)	**Rotel tomatoes,** with liquid
	White Stone-Ground Grits (see page 12)
6 large	**bell peppers,** topped, cored and seeded
I cup	**grated cheddar cheese**

Preheat oven to 375 degrees.

Brown onion in oil in a large pan. Add sirloin, garlic powder, onion powder, and salt and pepper. Cook meat through, then add tomatoes with liquid. Cook until liquid is reduced by half; remove from stove and fold in grits.

Coat the inside and outside of bell peppers with remaining oil, salt, and pepper. Stuff peppers with grit mixture and place on baking sheet. Bake for 20–30 minutes. For the last 5 minutes, top with cheddar cheese and cook until melted. Makes 6 servings.

GRITS & BLACK BEANS

2 cans (15 ounces each) **black beans**
2 teaspoons **cumin**
dash cayenne pepper
1 tablespoons **granulated sugar**
juice of 1 lime
White Stone-Ground Grits (see
page 12)
cilantro, for garnish

Drain and wash 1 can beans. Place beans into a nonstick pot and add
the other can with the liquid. Add all dry ingredients and lime juice.
Cook over medium heat until beans thicken, about 20 minutes. Spoon
over grits and garnish with cilantro. Makes 6 servings.

BIG R'S BARBECUE GRITS

Big R's Barbecue Sauce*:

2 cups	**ketchup**
I cup	**apple cider vinegar**
I cup	**water**
I teaspoon	**kosher salt**
I teaspoon	**black pepper**
I teaspoon	**cayenne pepper**
2 teaspoons	**chili powder**
$^1/_8$ cup	**brown sugar**

White Stone-Ground Grits (see page 12)
or **instant grits**

In a pot, simmer all sauce ingredients over low heat for I hour, stirring frequently. Fold barbecue sauce into cooked grits and enjoy. Makes 4–6 servings.

*Recipe courtesy of Randolph "Big R" Stafford, www.bigrbarbecue.com.

VIDALIA ONION CASSEROLE

4 tablespoons **vegetable oil**
3 **large Vidalia onions,** julienned
2 **eggs**
$^1/_2$ cup **chopped pickled jalapenos**
White Stone-Ground Grits (see page 12)
1 $^1/_2$ cups **sharp cheddar cheese**

Preheat oven to 350 degrees.

Heat a frying pan over high heat and add oil and onions; cook until onions are caramelized.

In a bowl, beat eggs and fold in onions and jalapenos. Add this mixture to cooked grits. Pour grits into a 9 x 13-inch baking dish and top with cheese. Bake for 35–40 minutes. Remove and serve with any meats and vegetables. Makes 6 servings.

VERY GARLICKY GRITS CASSEROLE

White Stone-Ground Grits (see page 12)
1 stick **unsalted butter,** softened (reserve 2 tablespoons for buttering baking dish)
2 **eggs,** beaten well
1 tube **garlic cheese**
$^1/_2$ cup **half-and-half**
$^1/_2$ cup **Nabisco cracker meal**
$^1/_2$ cup **crumbled corn flakes**

Preheat oven to 350 degrees.

In a bowl, mix together butter, eggs, cheese, and half-and-half. Fold into grits in three additions. Pour grits into a buttered 2-quart baking dish.

In a small bowl, mix together cracker meal and corn flakes. Top grits with this mixture. Bake for 20–30 minutes, or until top has browned nicely. Makes 6–8 servings.

PANHANDLE GRITS

I pound	**thick-cut bacon**
2 medium	**onions,** finely chopped
I	**green bell pepper,** diced
I	**red bell pepper,** diced
I ¹/₂ cups	**finely chopped country ham**
2 cans (I5 ounces each)	**Rotel tomatoes**
	White Stone-Ground Grits (see page I2)

In a frying pan, fry bacon and set aside. Saute onions and bell peppers in 2–3 tablespoons bacon drippings until browned. Add ham and stir well. Saute over medium-low heat for I5 minutes. Add tomatoes and simmer for 30 minutes. When grits are cooked, add ham mixture and stir well. Serve hot with bacon crumbled on top. Makes 8–I0 servings.

*Recipe concept from Coffee Cup Restaurant, Pensacola, Florida.

EXTRA CHEESE GRITS SOUFFLE

$^1/_2$ cup **grated extra sharp cheddar cheese**
$^1/_2$ cup **grated extra sharp white cheddar cheese**
  1 cup **melted butter**
      4 **eggs,** well beaten
$^1/_2$ cup **milk**
          kosher salt and pepper
          White Stone-Ground Grits (see page 12)

Preheat oven to 350 degrees.

Stir cheeses, butter, eggs, milk, salt, and pepper to taste into grits. Stir
until cheese is melted and milk has been absorbed. Pour into a buttered
3-quart baking dish and bake for 1 hour. Makes 8–10 servings.

BAKED GRUYERE
GRITS CASSEROLE

White Stone-Ground Grits (see page 12)
1 can (8 ounces) **Rotel tomatoes,** Italian blend
1 1/2 cups **grated Gruyere cheese**

Preheat oven to 350 degrees.

Pour grits into a greased baking dish and then top with tomatoes and cheese. Bake for 25 minutes, or until cheese has browned nicely. Makes 4 servings.

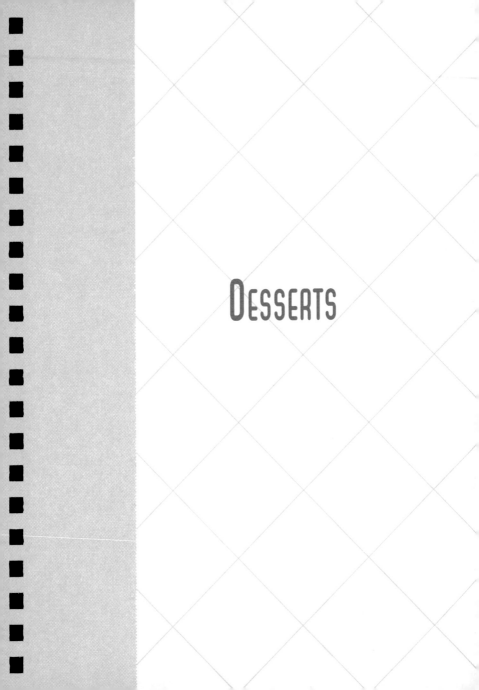

DESSERTS

CARAMEL GRITS

Sweet Vanilla Grits (see page 25)
I jar (12.25 ounces) **caramel sauce**
I cup **chopped pecans**
I pint **ice cream,** any flavor

Prepare grits according to recipe. Add caramel and mix well. Toast pecans and spoon over top of grits with ice cream. Makes 4 servings.

SOUTHERN CHOCOLATE GRITS TRUFFLES

Chocolate Grits (see page 26)
2 pounds **high-quality baker's milk chocolate,** divided

Prepare grits according to recipe or use instant grits and follow the package directions. (Stone ground grits offer a coarser texture, instant grits a smoother texture.) Chill for 2–4 hours or until set firm. Roll grits into $1/2$-inch balls. Place onto two parchment-lined sheet pans and refrigerate.

In a pot, heat $1/4$ inch water to boil. Chop chocolate into small pieces and place I pound chocolate into glass bowl. Place glass bowl over boiling water to create a double boiler. Melt chocolate until smooth. Remove one sheet pan from refrigerator. Submerge each truffle one at a time in melted chocolate, removing with fork and placing back on parchment. Repeat until all truffles are coated. Melt remaining chocolate as needed with double-boiler method. Makes 75 individual truffles.

VARIATION: Substitute white chocolate for milk chocolate.

VANILLA BEAN BRÛLÉE

Sweet Vanilla Grits (see page 25)
2 cups **granulated sugar**
1 **brûlée torch**
berries

Prepare grits according to recipe. Fill ramekins evenly with grits and chill 2 hours. Moisten ramekin tops with wet paper towel. Place sugar in a bowl. Spoon sugar over top of ramekin, coating the top of the grits evenly. Remove any excess sugar by flipping ramekin upside down in bowl. If not coated evenly, repeat. Caramelize sugar with torch and serve with fresh garden berries of your choice. Makes 6 servings.

*For a smoother texture, use instant grits.

WHITE CHOCOLATE BRÛLÉE

Sweet Vanilla Grits (see page 25)
1 bag (11 ounces) **Ghirardelli white chocolate chips**
2 cups **granulated sugar**
1 **brûlée torch**
berries

Prepare grits according to recipe. When finished, fold in white chocolate chips. Fill ramekins evenly and chill 3 hours. Moisten tops of ramekins with wet paper towel. Place sugar in a bowl. Spoon sugar over top of each ramekin, coating the tops of grits evenly. Remove any excess sugar by flipping ramekin upside down in bowl. If not coated evenly, repeat. Caramelize sugar with torch and serve with fresh garden berries of your choice. Makes 6 servings.

*For a smoother texture, use instant grits.

ESPRESSO GRITS BRÛLÉE

Espresso Grits (see page 31)*
2 cups **granulated sugar**
1 **brûlée torch**
berries

Prepare grits according to recipe. Fill ramekins evenly with grits and chill 2–3 hours. Moisten tops with wet paper towel. Place sugar in a large bowl. Spoon sugar over top of ramekins, coating top of grits evenly. Remove any excess sugar by flipping ramekin upside down in bowl. If not coated evenly, repeat. Caramelize sugar with torch and serve with fresh garden berries. Makes 6 servings.

*For a smoother texture, use instant grits.

CHOCOLATE GRITS AND SWEET WAFFLES

Chocolate Grits (see page 26)
4 **buttermilk waffles,** make them or buy frozen (see page 104)
1 pint **pistachio ice cream**

Prepare grits according to recipe and keep over low heat while preparing waffles. Place two sections of a waffle on a plate and top each with grits. Top with 1–2 scoops ice cream. Makes 8 servings.

BUTTERMILK WAFFLES

2	**eggs**
2 cups	**milk**
5 tablespoons	**vegetable oil**
3 cups	**flour**
3 teaspoons	**baking powder**
I teaspoon	**kosher salt**
2 teaspoons	**sugar**
I teaspoon	**baking soda**
I cup	**water**

In a bowl, beat eggs, milk, and oil together. In a separate bowl, mix flour, baking powder, salt, and sugar and then add egg mixture. Dissolve soda in water and add to batter; batter will be thin. You can keep the batter in the refrigerator for a few days. When you want to use it, just add a little extra baking powder and you're good to go. Fill waffle iron with batter and cook until golden brown. Serve with your choice of sweet flavored grits. Makes 8–10 servings.

ORANGE AND MAPLE CREAM PUDDING

1/2 cup	**packed brown sugar**
4 large	**eggs**
	zest of 2 oranges
1/3 cup	**fresh orange juice**
2 tablespoons	**unsalted butter**
1 tablespoon	**dark corn syrup**
1 tablespoon	**pure maple syrup**
1 tablespoon	**dark rum**
1/2 teaspoon	**salt**
1/2 teaspoon	**cinnamon**
1/2 teaspoon	**ground ginger**
1/2 teaspoon	**ground cloves**
	Sweet Vanilla Grits (see page 25)
1/2 cup	**chopped pecans**
1/4 cup	**dark brown sugar**
2 tablespoons	**unsalted butter**
	vanilla ice cream

Preheat oven to 350 degrees.

In a bowl, mix all ingredients together, except grits, pecans, dark brown sugar, 2 tablespoons unsalted butter, and ice cream, with an electric mixer until smooth. Add grits and mix to incorporate until well blended.

In a separate bowl, mix pecans, dark brown sugar, and 2 tablespoons unsalted butter and then set aside. Pour grit mixture into a buttered 9 x 13-inch baking dish and bake 25 minutes. Remove and top with pecan mixture; bake another 20 minutes, or until top is caramelized. Serve hot with ice cream. Makes 10–12 servings.

FRIED CHOCOLATE GRITS

Chocolate Grits (see page 26)
2 cups **flour**
1 tablespoon **cornstarch**
1 teaspoon **salt**
1 **cup sugar**
5 cups **vegetable oil**
ice cream

Prepare grits according to recipe. Pour into a 9 x 13-inch dish. Cool 2–3 hours. Cut grits into bite-size pieces or use cookie cutters to make varying shapes. Make any shape you want, but they should not be more than a bite or so.

In a bowl, mix together all dry ingredients. In a frying pan, heat oil. Bread grits in dry ingredient mixture and fry over medium-high heat until golden brown. Serve over your favorite ice cream. Makes 6–8 servings.

SEASONAL BERRY CREPE

sweet grits recipe (see pages 25–29)
I package **fresh crepes**
fresh berries

Prepare grits according to recipe. Fill crepes with grits and berries; roll
up and top with more berries. Serve hot or at room temperature. Makes
6–8 servings.

GRITS NEAPOLITAN

$^1/_2$ batch **Vanilla Grits** (see page 25)
$^1/_2$ batch **Strawberry Grits** (see page 29)
$^1/_2$ batch **Chocolate Grits** (see page 26)

Prepare grits according to recipes. Line a loaf pan with plastic wrap and layer vanilla grits, strawberry grits, and chocolate grits, let cool. Serve chilled or frozen. Makes 10–12 servings.

HAZELNUT TRIFLE

2 packages (3 ounces each) **ladyfingers,** quartered
I cup **raspberry liquor**
$^1/_2$ cup **cocoa powder,** for garnish
Hazelnut Grits (see page 28)
2 cups **whipped cream**
I pint **fresh raspberries**
I bag **mint**

Soak ladyfingers in raspberry liquor. Rim 6 deep martini glasses with extra liquor and coat with cocoa. Place some ladyfingers in the bottom of the glasses, top with grits and then whipped cream. Repeat layering until glasses are full. Chill and garnish with fresh raspberries and mint sprig. Makes 6 servings.

KEY LIME TRIFLE

zest of **2 limes**
Key Lime Grits (see page 30)
2 cups **crushed graham crackers**
2 cups **whipped cream**
juice of 1 key lime
6 **key lime slices,** for garnish

Fold lime zest into cooked grits. Rim 6 deep martini glasses with some
key lime juice and coat with some cracker crumbs. Place some cracker
crumbs in the bottom of each glass, top with a small amount of grits
and whipped cream, and repeat until filled. Chill and garnish with key
lime slices. Makes 6 servings.

HAZELNUT GRITS NAPOLEON

1/2 cup **hazelnuts**
1 package **Pillsbury Puff Pastry Dough**
1 **egg**
2 tablespoons **milk**
Hazelnut Grits (see page 28)
1 cup **whipped cream**
1 1/2 cups **fresh assorted berries,** sliced

Toast hazelnuts for about 6 minutes or until they become aromatic,
then place them in middle of a kitchen towel. Rub them together
aggressively to remove the skin. In a food processor or on a cutting
board, coarsely chop hazelnuts; set aside. Place puff pastry on a sheet
pan lined with parchment paper.

In a bowl, mix egg and milk well. Brush a small amount egg mixture
over dough and bake according to package directions. Cut pastry into 6
pieces and divide each piece into 3 by pulling apart from the top. Place
1 piece of pastry on a plate, top with grits, berries, and nuts. Place
another piece of pastry on top and repeat layering. Place the third piece
of pastry on top and add a dollop of whipped cream, berries, and nuts.
Makes 6 servings.

RUM RAISIN AND BANANA PORRIDGE

$^1/_2$ stick **unsalted butter**
1 cup **golden raisins**
$^1/_3$ cup **dark rum**
$^1/_2$ cup **packed brown sugar**
2 ripe **bananas,** sliced in small pieces
Sweet Vanilla Grits (see page 25)

Heat frying pan over medium-high heat, add butter and let foam dissipate. Add raisins and cook for 3 minutes. Add rum and then reduce by half; add sugar. Let sugar melt and add bananas. Cook for 2 minutes in sugar and remove from heat. Top grits with rum-raisin mixture. Makes 4–6 servings.

TIRAMISU

6 **egg yolks**
1 cup **sugar**
³/₄ cup **Sweet Vanilla Grits** (see page 25)
1 cup **mascarpone cheese**
3 **egg whites**
¹/₂ cup **cold espresso**
¹/₄ cup **rum**
2 packages (3 ounces each) **ladyfingers**
cocoa powder

In a bowl, combine egg yolks and sugar, beating until light and creamy with an electric mixer. Fold grits into cheese in two additions. Add grit mixture to egg mixture 3 tablespoons at a time until smooth and creamy.

In a separate bowl beat egg whites until stiff peaks form. (Be careful not to use a bowl with any oil residue because the egg whites will not stiffen.) Fold in the grit mixture in three or four additions.

In a small bowl, mix espresso and rum. Separate the ladyfingers and place them in a 9-inch-square baking pan. Evenly soak ladyfingers with half the espresso mixture and then top with grit mixture and repeat. Dust top with cocoa powder and chill at least 3 hours. Makes 6 servings.

STRAWBERRY SHORTCAKES

2¹/₂ cups **chopped fresh strawberries**
1 cup **sugar**
1 **angel food cake**
2 cups **whipped cream**
Strawberry Grits (see page 29)
mint sprigs

In a bowl, combine strawberries and sugar and refrigerate for 2 hours to form strawberry liquor. Slice angel food cake in 4 uniform slices across the top to make layers. Spread some whipped cream across the bottom and top with grits and strawberries, drizzling some of the juices on top. Repeat; once all 4 layers are finished, top cake with the remaining berries and cream. Garnish each serving with mint. Makes 8 servings.

CHOCOLATE CREAM CHEESE CAKE

I box	**chocolate cake mix**
4	**eggs**
$^1/_2$ cup	**melted butter**
I cup	**uncooked instant grits**
I $^1/_2$ cups	**powdered sugar**
I package (8 ounces)	**cream cheese**
I teaspoon	**vanilla**
$^1/_3$ cup	**flour**
I pint	**vanilla ice cream**
I pint	**fresh raspberries**

Preheat oven to 350 degrees.

In a bowl, mix cake mix, 2 eggs, butter, and grits.

In a separate bowl, use an electric mixer to beat together remaining eggs, powdered sugar, cream cheese, and vanilla until smooth. Grease a 9 x 13-inch cake pan and sprinkle with flour to coat the pan, discard extra flour. Spread the cake mix in the pan and top with the cream cheese mixture. Bake 45 minutes, or until a toothpick is inserted and comes out clean. Top with ice cream and raspberries. Makes 9 servings.

GRITS WITH TART GRANNY SMITH APPLES

1 cup	**heavy cream**
2 cups	**milk**
2 teaspoons	**ground cinnamon**
1/2 teaspoon	**vanilla**
1/2 cup	**granulated sugar**
3/4 cups	**uncooked instant grits**
1 teaspoon	**salt**
3	**Granny Smith apples**
1/3 cup	**packed brown sugar**
3 tablespoons	**unsalted butter**
1 jar (12.25 ounces)	**caramel sauce**

Heat a nonstick pot to medium-low heat. Add cream, milk, cinnamon, vanilla, and sugar. Bring to boil and add grits and salt. Cook on low heat for 35–40 minutes, or until grits have absorbed the liquid. Stir grits occasionally. Grease six 1 cup ramekins. Spoon grits into ramekins and refrigerate overnight.

Before serving, peel apples and slice into thin slivers. In a bowl, mix together apples and brown sugar. Heat a large frying pan to medium-high, add butter and cook apples until sugar has melted and apples have browned. Heat caramel sauce in microwave, place ramekins in the microwave and heat for no more than 20 seconds, grits may fall because of cream. Serve grits with caramel and apples. Makes 6 servings.

STRAWBERRY GRITS
WITH BALSAMIC REDUCTION

1 pint **balsamic vinegar**
$^1/_2$ cup **sugar**
Strawberry Grits (see page 29)
2 cups **sliced fresh strawberries**

In a 4-quart pot, bring vinegar and sugar to a boil and reduce heat to
medium high. Simmer until it has reduced by three-fourths and has
become a syrup. Serve grits topped with fresh berries and balsamic
reduction. Makes 6 servings.

Hominy Grits

BOILED HOMINY

I can (15.5 ounces) **white hominy**
3 cups **chicken stock**
¹/₃ cup **distilled vinegar**
kosher salt

In a pot, combine hominy, stock, vinegar, and salt to taste. Boil for I
hour or more, stirring frequently to avoid lumps. Makes 4–6 servings.

*Adapted from *The Savannah Cook Book,* by Harriet Ross Colquitt, 1933.

FRIED HOMINY

2 cans (15.5 ounces each)	**white hominy**
2	**eggs**
1 log (8 ounces)	**goat cheese**
	kosher salt and pepper
$^1/_4$ cup	**oil,** or as needed
1 cup	**Nabisco cracker meal**

On a platter, spread out the hominy, about 1 inch thick to get it cold.
Slice this cold mixture into any shape desired. In a bowl, beat eggs and
cheese together; salt and pepper to taste. Roll mixture first in eggs,
then in cracker meal to coat. Heat oil in a frying pan over medium-high
heat and fry hominy. Makes 4–6 servings.

*Adapted from *The Savannah Cook Book*, by Harriet Ross Colquitt, 1933.

HOMINY CASSEROLE

2 cups **cold hominy**
1 1/2 cups **grated white cheddar cheese**
2 bunches **scallions,** chopped
2 **eggs,** well beaten
1 tablespoon **butter**
2 cups **milk**
kosher salt

Preheat oven to 350 degrees. Mash cold hominy well to remove the lumps. Fold in 1 cup cheese and scallions. Add eggs, butter, milk, and salt to taste. Put in a buttered 9 x 13-inch baking dish, top with remaining cheese, and bake for 40 minutes. Makes 4–6 servings.

*Adapted from *The Savannah Cook Book*, by Harriet Ross Colquitt, 1933.

SOUTHWEST BAKED HOMINY

2 cans (15.5 ounces each) **white hominy**
I large **sweet onion,** chopped
2 cups **sour cream**
I¹/₂ cups **grated pepper jack cheese**
I can (4.5 ounces) **chopped green chiles**
2 **eggs**
kosher salt to taste
4 teaspoons **butter**
I cup **Nabisco cracker meal**

Preheat oven to 350 degrees. In a bowl, mix first seven ingredients.
Grease a 9 x 13-inch baking dish with 2 tablespoons butter and add
mixture. Top with cracker meal. Cut remaining butter into small pieces
and spread across the top. Bake for 35 minutes or until browned on
top. Makes 6 servings.

NOTES

NOTES

NOTES

ABOUT THE AUTHOR

A true southerner living in Greenville, South Carolina, Harriss Cottingham knows grits. His passion for food began as a young boy while taste-testing for his grandfather who was an amateur chef.

Harriss Cottingham learned the culinary arts at Johnson and Wales University Culinary School in Charleston, South Carolina, and has worked in several fine dining restaurants. Now a sales representative for a wine distributor, he owns and operates Catering by Harriss, featuring cooking classes and small-group events.